THE SPY GAME

INTERNATIONAL AND MILITARY INTELLIGENCE

THE SPY GAME

INTERNATIONAL AND MILITARY INTELLIGENCE

EDITED BY LIONEL PENDER

Britannica
Educational Publishing

IN ASSOCIATION WITH

ROSEN
EDUCATIONAL SERVICES

Published in 2017 by Britannica Educational Publishing (a trademark of Encyclopædia Britannica, Inc.) in association with The Rosen Publishing Group, Inc.
29 East 21st Street, New York, NY 10010

Distributed exclusively by Rosen Publishing.
To see additional Britannica Educational Publishing titles, go to rosenpublishing.com.

First Edition

Britannica Educational Publishing
J.E. Luebering: Executive Director, Core Editorial
Anthony L. Green: Editor, Compton's by Britannica

Rosen Publishing
Lionel Pender: Editor
Nelson Sá: Art Director
Brian Garvey: Designer
Cindy Reiman: Photography Manager
Bruce Donnola: Photo Researcher
Introduction and conclusion by Michael Ray.

Library of Congress Cataloging-in-Publication Data

Names: Pender, Lionel.
Title: The spy game : international and military intelligence / Edited by Lionel Pender.
Description: New York, NY : Britannica Educational Publishing, 2017. |
  Series: Law enforcement and intelligence gathering
  | Includes bibliographical references and index.
Identifiers: LCCN 2016020889 | ISBN 9781508103707 (library bound : alk. paper)
Subjects: LCSH: Intelligence service--Juvenile literature. |
  Espionage--Juvenile literature. | Spies--Juvenile literature.
Classification: LCC JF1525.I6 S79 2017 | DDC 327.12--dc23
LC record available at https://lccn.loc.gov/2016020889

Manufactured in China

Photo credits: Cover, p. 3 Ryan Etter/Ikon Images/Getty Images; pp. 8–9 (background), 11, 28, 45, 67 hunthomas/Shutterstock.com; p. 9 Paul J. Richards/AFP/Getty Image; p. 13 Pete Souza - Official White House Photo; p. 14, 16, 52 © AP Images; pp. 20–21 DigitalGlobe/ScapeWare3d/Getty Images; pp. 24–25 John Moore/Getty Images; pp. 26–27 Stephen Chernin/Getty Images; p. 29 Private Collection/© Look and Learn/Bridgeman Images; p. 33 Hulton Archive/Getty Images; p. 34 Staatliche Museen zu Berlin—Preussischer Kulturbesitz; p. 36 National Archives, Washington, DC; pp. 40–41 © Everett Collection Inc/Alamy Stock Photo; p. 42–43 © 1964 United Artists Corporation with Eon Productions; p. 47 FBI; p. 48–49 Glowimages/Getty Images; p. 54 Nikolai Malyshev/AFP/Getty Images; p. 56 Oli Scarff/Getty Images; p. 60 © epa european pressphoto agency b.v./Alamy Stock Photo; p. 62–63 Barry Iverson/The LIFE Images Collection/Getty Images; p. 65 Jiji Press/AFP/GettyImages; p. 68–69 Ali Yussef/AFP/Getty Images; p. 72–73 Courtesy Photo/U.S. Air Force; p. 75 ullstein bild/Getty Images; p. 80 Encyclopædia Britannica, Inc.; p. 82–83 Air Accidents Investigation Branch, United Kingdom/Contains public sector information licensed under the Open Government Licence v3.0; p. 86–87 Alain Mingam/Gamma-Rapho/Getty Images; back cover, interior pages (background) stefano carniccio/Shutterstock.com

36242060439466

CONTENTS

INTRODUCTION

Leaders of all kinds seek to obtain intelligence, or secret information, to achieve an advantage over their opponents. Heads of government, presidents of companies, and even managers of sports teams try to acquire information that would give them insight into the intentions or weaknesses of their adversaries. In this book, we will examine the development of intelligence gathering as a discipline and the growth of national intelligence agencies around the world.

Any discussion of spies naturally conjures images of James Bond and clandestine operations conducted with high-tech gadgets. Field agents certainly do have a role in the gathering of intelligence, although few would likely aspire to a job as action-packed as 007's. The life of a clandestine agent is fraught with danger, as evidenced by the Memorial Wall at the original headquarters building of the US Central Intelligence Agency (CIA) in Langley, Virginia. The wall is covered with scores of stars, one for each agent who lost his or her life in the line of duty. While many of the agents' names are listed in a "book of honor" that accompanies the memorial, some names remain secret to this day.

Risk has always accompanied the job of the field agent. During the American Revolution, American officer Nathan Hale was executed by the British as a spy, while British officer John André was executed by the Americans. The inherent danger of intelligence gathering prompted countries and their militaries to develop

While the thought of spies often brings to mind the action-packed scenes of Hollywood movies, in reality intelligence gathering often occurs behind closed doors in agency headquarters.

strategies that—in theory—would minimize the possibility of harm to their own assets while maintaining a watchful eye on their enemies. Technology has come to play an enormous role in these efforts. The Space Race saw the United States and the Soviet Union jockeying for orbital advantage, with satellites offering a real-time glimpse of events on the ground. No longer would analysts be forced to wait for sensitive sites to be photographed by spies on the ground or glimpsed by reconnaissance aircraft—a camera thousands of miles above Earth could deliver crisp images of actions as they transpired.

This sort of tactical data can be invaluable, but even the best raw intelligence is worthless without informed analysis. A pair of US Army Signal Corps radar operators detected the first wave of Japanese bombers approaching Pearl Harbor nearly an hour before the attack began on the morning of December 7, 1941. They notified their information center, but the officer on duty disregarded the warning, believing the planes to be a squadron of American bombers approaching from the mainland. The proliferation of computer technology has certainly aided in the handling and analysis of intelligence, with the US Defense Advanced Research Projects Agency (DARPA) going so far as to propose an initiative titled "Total Information Awareness." The goal of the program was to create an all-encompassing surveillance network, with computers performing threat analysis on all electronic communication and digital traffic. The program was officially discontinued after a flurry of media criticism, but many elements of it were preserved by the National Security Agency (NSA). For a time the NSA, jokingly referred to as "No Such Agency" because of the intense secrecy surrounding its operations, reportedly intercepted billions of emails, data transmissions, and phone records every day. With this staggering volume of data streaming in around the clock, one is forced to consider if there could be such a thing as too much intelligence.

CHAPTER ONE

NATURE OF INTELLIGENCE

ntelligence, in government and military operations, is evaluated information about the strength, activities, and probable courses of action of foreign countries or non-state actors that are usually—although not always—enemies. The term is also used to refer to the collection, analysis, and distribution of such information and also to secret intervention in the political affairs of other countries, an activity commonly known as "covert action." Intelligence is an important component of national power and an essential element in decision making regarding national security, defense, and foreign policies.

LEVELS OF INTELLIGENCE

Intelligence is conducted on three levels: strategic (sometimes called national), tactical, and counter-intelligence. The broadest of these levels is strategic intelligence. Strategic intelligence includes information about what foreign countries have the capability to do and their general intentions. Tactical intelligence (which is sometimes called operational or combat intelligence) is information required by military field commanders. Because of the destructive power of modern weapons, the decision making of world leaders must often consider information derived from tactical as well as strategic intelligence. Military commanders, too, may often need multiple levels of intelligence. As a result, the distinction between these two types of intelligence may be diminishing.

Counterintelligence is intelligence aimed at protecting a country's intelligence operations and keeping them secret. Its purpose is to prevent spies or other foreign agents from infiltrating the country's government, military, or intelligence agencies. Counterintelligence is also concerned with protecting advanced technology, preventing terrorism, and combating international drug trafficking. Counterintelligence operations sometimes produce positive intelligence, including information about other countries' intelligence-gathering tools and techniques and about the kinds of intelligence other countries are seeking. Counterintelligence sometimes involves the use of "moles," or double agents, to manipulate an adversary's intelligence services. In authoritarian states (where a single power holder, such as a dictator or military group, controls all aspects of the government), counterintelligence commonly entails the surveillance of key elites and the repression of dissent.

Governments often use their intelligence agencies to carry out covert actions to support diplomatic initiatives or to achieve goals unattainable by diplomatic means

World leaders, such as US president Barack Obama *(seated second from left)*, must evaluate strategic and tactical intelligence before making decisions regarding military action, as in the Osama bin Laden mission of May 2011.

alone. The US Central Intelligence Agency (CIA), for example, organized the overthrow of the government of Guatemala by military coup in 1954. It also helped to undermine the government of President Salvador Allende of Chile prior to the military coup there in 1973. More recently, US covert actions have included

Chilean president Salvador Allende speaks before the United Nations General Assembly in New York, NY, in 1972. The CIA undermined his government for years before he was ousted by a military coup in 1973.

providing military and financial support to the muja-hideen—Islamic fundamentalists who fought Soviet troops in Afghanistan during the 1980s—and aiding US and British military forces in their campaign against Afghanistan's Taliban government in 2001. Earlier in the twentieth century, the intelligence services of the Soviet Union assassinated exiled political figures such as Leon Trotsky and supported Marxist-Leninist organizations throughout the world.

TYPES OF INTELLIGENCE

The types of intelligence a country may require are varied. A country's armed services need military intelligence; its space and Earth-satellite programs need scientific intelligence; its foreign offices need political intelligence; and its head of government needs a combination of many kinds of intelligence.

Because of these varied needs, intelligence has become a vast industry. At the start of the twenty-first century, it was estimated that the US government spent some $30 billion each year on intelligence-related activities. US intelligence agencies were estimated to employ about 200,000 people domestically and many thousands more abroad in intelligence-gathering activities. The intelligence operations of the Soviet Union were likely of even greater dimensions prior to the dissolution

US ambassador to China Jon Huntsman (left) stands with President Barack Obama during a state visit to China in 2009. World leaders often collect political intelligence from high-ranking diplomats abroad.

of the country in 1991. All other major countries also maintain large intelligence agencies.

Political intelligence is both the most sought-after and the least reliable of the various types of intelligence. Because no one can predict with absolute certainty the effects of the political forces in a foreign country, analysts can merely predict possible courses of action based on what is known about political trends. Concrete data that are helpful in this regard include voting trends, details of political party organization and leadership, and information from political documents. Political intelligence has long been gathered from the reports of diplomats, who normally collect data from "open," or legally accessible, sources in the country where they are stationed. Their work is supplemented by that of professional intelligence agents.

Much military intelligence is gathered by military attachés, who have formal diplomatic status but are known to be mainly concerned with intelligence. Space satellites produce reliable information about the makeup of military units and weapons and can track their movements. Satellites are especially important for monitoring a country's production of long-range missiles and weapons of mass destruction (biological, chemical, and nuclear weapons). The most valuable kinds of military intelligence concern military organization and equipment, procedures and formations, and the number of units and total personnel.

THE PROBLEM OF MOLES

Perhaps the most serious threat to an intelligence agency is the double agent, commonly called a counterspy, or mole. A mole works for an agency in his or her native country but also, secretly, for the agency of an unfriendly nation.

Every major agency has had its moles, and some of them have done great disservice to the countries of their pretended loyalty. Probably the most notorious mole in modern history was Harold A. R. "Kim" Philby, who—with his associates Guy Burgess, Donald Maclean, and Anthony Blunt—cooperated secretly for years with Soviet Union intelligence while working for the British intelligence agency, MI6. While serving as the top liaison officer between the British and US intelligence services in the 1940s and early 1950s, Philby gave detailed information about MI6 and the Central Intelligence Agency (CIA) to the Soviets. He also disclosed to the Soviet Union an Allied plan to send armed anticommunist bands into Albania in 1950, which assured their defeat. In 1963, fearful of being found out, Philby defected to the Soviet Union, where Burgess and Maclean had fled some years earlier.

In the 1990s, two high-ranking CIA officials were arrested for selling US intelligence information to the Soviet Union and Russia. The first was Aldrich Ames, who had sold American intelligence information to the Soviets throughout the 1980s. At least ten CIA agents within the Soviet Union were executed as a result of Ames's spying;

ultimately, he revealed the name of every US agent operating in the Soviet Union (after 1991, Russia). In 1996 the FBI apprehended Harold J. Nicholson, who had joined the CIA in 1980, and accused him of spying for Russia since 1994. According to the FBI, Nicholson sold the names of CIA agents operating in Russia to the Russian government. The motivation for both officials' betrayal was monetary and in no way ideologically charged. Nicholson was the highest-ranking CIA official ever to be arrested for espionage.

The state of a country's economy greatly affects its military strength, its political developments, and its foreign policy. For that reason, the collection of economic information, including data on trade, finance, natural resources, industrial capacity, and gross national product, is of great importance to intelligence agencies.

Because technology is continually advancing, there are always new methods of collecting intelligence and new techniques for protecting secret information. To guard against scientific or technological breakthroughs that may give other countries an advantage, intelligence organizations try to stay aware of foreign advances in nuclear technology, in the electronic, chemical, and computer sciences, and in many other scientific fields.

In order to make accurate predictions of a foreign country's future behavior, intelligence agencies also require detailed information about the personal characteristics of the country's leaders. Intelligence agencies also collect data on foreign populations, topographies, climates, and a wide range of ecological factors.

SOURCES OF INTELLIGENCE

Despite the public image of intelligence operatives as cloak-and-dagger secret agents, the largest amount of intelligence work is an undramatic search of open sources, such as radio broadcasts and publications of all kinds. Much of this work, which includes sifting through reports from diplomats, businessmen, military attachés, and other observers, is performed by university-trained research analysts in quiet offices.

Covert sources of intelligence fall into three major categories. They are imagery intelligence, which includes air and space reconnaissance; signals intelligence, which includes electronic eavesdropping and code breaking; and human intelligence, which involves the secret agent working at the classic spy trade.

DigitalGlobe / 38 North
February 16, 2016

pport building

Test cell

stand with
ort tower

Heavy construction
crane

building

An air reconnaissance mission captured this photograph of North Korea's submarine-based ballistic missile program in February 2016. Such reconnaissance photographs fall into the category of imagery intelligence.

Broadly speaking, the relative value of these sources is reflected in the order in which they are listed here. A photograph, for example, constitutes hard (that is, reliable) intelligence. In turn, the report of a secret agent may be speculative and difficult to prove.

METHODS OF INTELLIGENCE GATHERING

Good intelligence management begins with properly determining what needs to be known. Unless this step is done first, data will be collected unsystematically, making it difficult for the decision maker to choose an appropriate course of action. Collected data must be evaluated and transformed into a usable form (and sometimes stored for future use). Evaluation is essential, because many sources turn out to be unreliable. A system must be used to rate how reliable sources are and how accurate the information they provide is.

Information gathered from open sources probably makes up more than four-fifths of intelligence gathered, though this estimate varies with the number of state secrets a country may have. Clandestine collection methods involving undercover sources provide the basis for much of the drama and romance associated with intelligence work in fiction. Although classic espionage agents have not become wholly obsolete, their role largely has been taken over by machines, including reconnaissance satellites, long-range cameras, and various sensing, detecting, and acoustical instruments. With technological advances, it has become possible to see in darkness, to hear from great distances, and to take detailed photographs from heights of hundreds of miles. Nevertheless, only human spies can gather information about the attitudes and intentions of foreign leaders or international terrorists and other criminals. Indeed, some critics cited a lack of human intelligence as a factor in the failure of US intelligence agencies to prevent the terrorist attacks of September 11, 2001.

Techniques of aerial reconnaissance—intelligence collected by air- and spacecraft—have advanced greatly since the 1940s, when the United States drifted balloons carrying special cameras across Soviet territory to photograph military and industrial sites. Today, aerial reconnaissance is carried out by satellites, aircraft, and unmanned drones, which can orbit a battlefield for twenty-four hours. The US U-2 aircraft and its higher-flying successors can take photographs that experts can read with great accuracy. Imaging satellites, which can produce accurate information about the number and location of a country's nuclear missiles and other weapons, made possible the arms control treaties between the United States and the Soviet Union. High-altitude photographs are also used to diagnose environmental catastrophes, to locate terrorist training camps, and even to detect human rights abuses.

Unmanned drones, such as this US Air Force MQ-1B Predator, have become an important tool for aerial reconnaissance. They can orbit a battlefield and collect intelligence without risking the lives of human pilots.

Intelligence organizations often employ electronic scavengers (from ships, planes, listening posts in embassies and military installations, and orbiting satellites) to collect information about a country's radio communications and its naval equipment and operations. An individual submarine, for example, can be

identified by the telltale and unique noises it makes (its "signature"). During the Cold War, the United States collected sensitive signals intelligence by tapping communications lines in Soviet territorial waters. It also used satellites and special planes for conducting missions close to the borders of potential adversaries. Similarly, the Soviet Union (and later Russia) collected signals intelligence from listening stations in diplomatic and consular missions and from large "fishing trawlers" that shadowed the US fleet.

The use of computers to analyze data on complex phenomena such as industrial production, missile launches, and rates of economic growth has created vast amounts of information that threaten to overwhelm intelligence systems. Therefore, the filtering of useless information has become a key task. Since World War II, great efforts have been made to develop efficient means of cataloging, storing, and retrieving the gigantic volume of data being collected. Although some observers believe that data collection, especially in the internet age, has been overemphasized at the expense of analysis, computer technology and the application of artificial

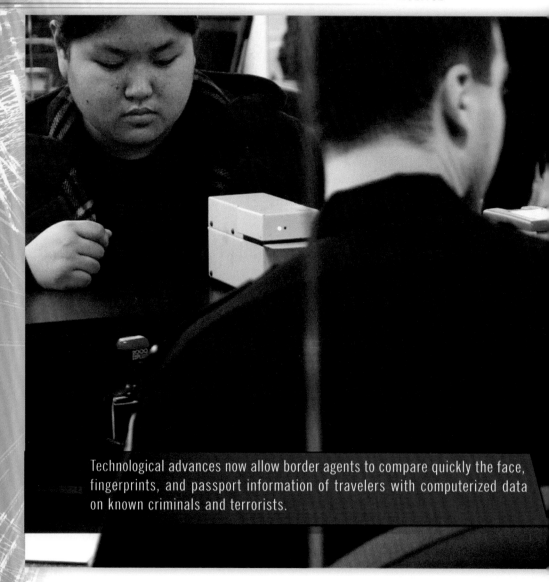

Technological advances now allow border agents to compare quickly the face, fingerprints, and passport information of travelers with computerized data on known criminals and terrorists.

intelligence, which allow computer programs to organize large amounts of raw data for analysts, promise to make such large quantities of information manageable. For example, such techniques can be used

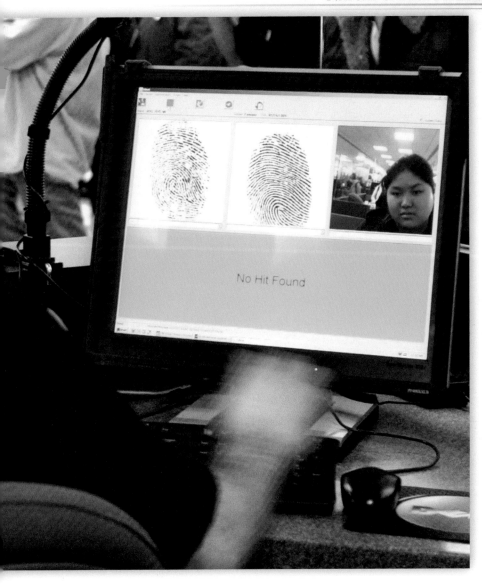

No Hit Found

at border crossings to quickly compare the image of a suspected terrorist with thousands of pictures of known criminals.

CHAPTER TWO

HISTORY OF INTELLIGENCE ACTIVITIES

Since ancient times, military and political leaders have understood the value of intelligence to inform their decisions. In the modern era, means of surveillance and intelligence have benefitted much from technological advances, leading to greater quantities and accuracy of data.

PREMODERN INTELLIGENCE

The Bible says that God advised Moses (Numbers 13) to send agents to "spy out the land of Canaan." In the Book of Joshua, when the Israelites were about to conquer Palestine, their leader Joshua sent two spies out

Intelligence gathering is not a modern development. Illustrated here is the biblical scene in which spies sent by Moses return after scouting out the land of Canaan for the Israelites.

"secretly with orders to reconnoiter the country." This happened earlier than 1200 BCE.

The ancient Chinese military strategist Sunzi, who lived in the fifth century BCE, penned *Bingfa* (*The Art of War*). The text, which is said to be widely read by contemporary Chinese strategists, stressed the importance of good intelligence organization. He also wrote of counterintelligence and psychological warfare.

In Europe during the Middle Ages, intelligence was systematically used but crudely organized. Although it was usually impossible to conceal the massing of troops or ships, communication was slow, making

SUNZI AND
THE ART OF WAR

In his classic text *The Art of War*, Sunzi identified five kinds of secret agent. The first has its modern counterpart in the agent in place, an agent who has access to enemy secrets. The second is today's double agent, or mole, who is recruited from an enemy's intelligence agency. The third, the modern-day deception agent, provides purposefully incorrect information to confuse the enemy. The fourth is the expendable agent, whose loss allows other more important agents to operate. The fifth and final of Sunzi's secret agents is the penetration agent, who has access to an enemy's senior leadership.

the achievement of strategic surprise a difficult matter of balancing the time required to assemble large forces against the time needed by enemy agents to discover and report them.

In the fifteenth century, the Italian city-states began to establish permanent embassies in foreign capitals. The Venetians used such outposts as sources of intelligence. They even developed codes and ciphers by which information could be secretly communicated. By the sixteenth century, other European governments were doing the same.

INTELLIGENCE AND THE RISE OF NATIONALISM

With the rise of nationalism came the growth of standing armies and professional diplomats as well as the establishment of organizations and methods for obtaining foreign intelligence. Queen Elizabeth I (reigned 1558–1603) of England maintained a notable intelligence organization. Her principal state secretary, Sir Francis Walsingham, developed a network of intelligence agents in foreign countries. He recruited graduates of Oxford and Cambridge, developed the craft of espionage (including tools and techniques for making and breaking codes), and engaged in much foreign political intrigue. Later, in the 1600s, Cardinal Richelieu of France and Oliver Cromwell of England—whose intelligence chief, John Thurloe, is

SIR FRANCIS WALSINGHAM, THE QUEEN'S "SPYMASTER"

Sir Francis Walsingham was an English statesman and diplomat notable for assembling an extensive spy network in Europe. He was secretary of state from 1573 to 1590 during the reign of Queen Elizabeth I.

As secretary of state, Walsingham made a point of collecting and mastering great amounts of information concerning government administration, economics, and practical politics. His far-flung network of spies and news gatherers spanned France, Scotland, the Low Countries, Spain, Italy, and even Turkey and North Africa. Walsingham secured the services of prison informants and double agents through bribery, veiled threats, and subtle psychological maneuvers.

Walsingham used his agents to infiltrate English Catholic circles in England and abroad, particularly among Mary Stuart's friends and agents in Scotland and France and at the Catholic seminaries established in Rome and Douai for training English priests. He eventually was provided £2,000 a year by the government to pay for these secret activities. Walsingham also employed experts on codes and ciphers and in the art of lifting the wax seal of a letter so that it could be undetectably opened and read. Through his agents, he received full data on the Spanish Armada before it sailed in 1588, thus enabling England to prepare to meet it. Walsingham was knighted in 1577.

Sir Francis Walsingham

THE ZIMMERMANN NOTE

The "Zimmermann Note" was a sensational proposal made to Mexico by German statesman Arthur Zimmermann during World War I. It was a secret telegram asking Mexico to enter into an alliance with Germany against the United States. The interception and decoding of the telegram by British intelligence was one of the most notable events in intelligence during the war.

Zimmermann wanted to nullify or at least reduce US intervention in the European war. To accomplish this, he planned to engage American arms and energies elsewhere by entangling the United States in war with Mexico and

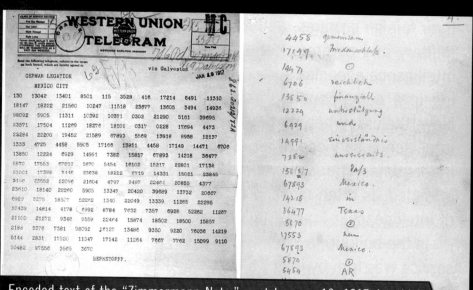

Encoded text of the "Zimmermann Note," sent January 16, 1917, in which Germany proposed a military alliance with Mexico against the United States

Japan. In pursuit of this goal, on January 16, 1917, he sent a secret telegram in code (through the German ambassador in Washington, DC) to the German minister in Mexico, authorizing him to propose an alliance to Mexico's president Venustiano Carranza. The offer included "an understanding on our part that Mexico is to reconquer her lost territory in Texas, New Mexico, and Arizona" (territory the United States had gained following the Mexican-American War of the mid-1800s). Carranza was also asked to "invite the immediate adherence of Japan." Intercepted and decoded by British Admiralty intelligence, the telegram was made available to US president Woodrow Wilson, who caused it to be published on March 1, 1917. In convincing Americans of German hostility toward the United States, the Zimmermann Note became one of the principal factors leading to the declaration of war by the United States against Germany five weeks later.

German military strength in 1914. German intelligence also had deteriorated. Nonetheless, the Germans carried out successful intelligence activities in Persia and scored limited successes in the United States. The Russian intelligence service initially enjoyed great success against the Austrians because of the treason of an Austrian general staff officer. However, it subsequently performed no better than the services of other countries involved in the war. The British succeeded in breaking German naval codes, and they were able to use the information they obtained to hasten US entry into the war by exposing German efforts to involve Mexico in a war with the United States. However, tactical intelligence provided to British commanders on the Western Front was full of optimistic and misleading assessments of Germany's military capabilities.

Unlike the European countries, the United States had no central intelligence organization. Indeed, at the start of the war, army intelligence was only a small section of the general staff—just two officers and two clerks. By the end of the war, this service had grown to 1,200 officers and civilians. Overall, the American intelligence community at this time was staffed by amateurs and was quite deficient.

The intelligence lessons of World War I, along with advances in technology—especially electronics and aircraft technology—resulted in the birth of new intelligence agencies in the 1920s and 1930s, particularly in Italy, Germany, and the Soviet Union. The expansionist interests of these three countries as well as Japan in the 1930s, and especially the outbreak of World War II in 1939, brought about the creation and growth of intelligence agencies throughout the world.

World War II imposed intelligence needs never before faced by the major warring powers, mainly as a result of quickly advancing military technology. Air warfare in particular required vast new intelligence operations.

Air force commanders needed information on possible bombing targets, as well as on enemy fighters and anti-aircraft artillery. In the first days of the war, the United States relied on the insurance records of German industries and on aerial reconnaissance to identify bombing targets. The growth of radio broadcasting gave way to the new art of psychological warfare, the effects of which intelligence services studied. In 1942, the United States created its first full-fledged organization for intelligence and secret operations, the Office of Strategic Services (OSS).

Yet despite its rapid development, intelligence forecasting remained a precarious trade. Many key events in the war—including the German invasion of the Soviet Union in June 1941, the Pearl Harbor attack against the United States by Japan in December 1941, the Battle of the Bulge in December 1944–January 1945, and the Allied bombing campaigns against Germany (1942–45), in which the Germans showed unexpected resilience—were marked by the failure of decision makers to profit from their elaborate intelligence networks.

However, there was one area of enormous success. Perhaps the most significant intelligence achievement of the war was the Ultra project, in which the British, using a German Enigma encoding machine obtained from the Poles and relying on earlier decryption efforts by the Poles and the French, intercepted and deciphered top-secret German military communications

US soldiers participate in an OSS training class at Milton Hall in Cambridgeshire, England, in 1944. These trainees would participate in Operation Jedburgh, a clandestine operation undertaken by the Allies during World War II.

throughout much of the war. In essence, the Ultra project enabled the Allies to read the mind of the German high command. As the war progressed, Hitler's increasingly centralized control of operations on all fronts made German military operations especially

vulnerable. Ultra was particularly import- ant in the defeat of the German U-boat fleet and the German surface navy. When the Allies were caught by surprise, such as in the American defeat at Kasserine Pass, the Allied defeat at Arnhem, and the Battle of the Bulge, the Germans had used land- lines for communication or Ultra intercepts had been misused.

During the Cold War, intelligence became one of the world's largest industries, employ- ing hundreds of thousands of professionals. Every major country created enormous new intelligence bureaucracies, often consisting of interlocking and competitive secret agen- cies that fought for new assignments and sometimes withheld information from each other. The United States established the Central Intelligence Agency (CIA) in 1947. Among other well-known intelligence orga- nizations created during this period were the United Kingdom's MI5 and MI6, the Soviet Union's KGB (Committee for State Security), France's SDECE (External Docu- mentation and Counterespionage Service), China's MSS (Ministry of State Security), and Israel's Mossad.

By the 1970s, every regional power and many rela- tively small states had developed intelligence services.

During the 1960s and 1970s, the spy genre became a staple of films, television, and books. James Bond, a character from the spy novels of Ian Fleming, was played by Sean Connery in the 1964 film *Goldfinger*.

At the same time, the exploits of spies and counterspies became a staple of the entertainment and publishing industries. In books, movies, and television, intelligence agents were portrayed in roles that were

sometimes comic but often deadly serious. All these accounts tended to glamorize an occupation that was often painfully tedious and sometimes (in the opinion of some) distasteful and immoral.

In the last two decades of the Cold War, the United States relied heavily on imagery and signals intelligence, including satellite photography, to collect information on Soviet weapons of mass destruction. Its emphasis on these sources of intelligence, however, may actually have weakened its ability to combat terrorist organizations, which by their nature are not easily penetrated through technical means.

Since the break-up of the Soviet Union and the end of the Cold War, non-state actors such as terrorist organizations, militias, and drug cartels have developed sophisticated intelligence capabilities that rival those of some states. The Islamic terrorist organization al-Qaeda, which organized the September 11 attacks against the United States, had an intelligence infrastructure that maintained safe houses in the Middle East, Europe, and North America. Evidence uncovered after the US and British military campaign in Afghanistan indicated that al-Qaeda had purchased sophisticated computer hardware that allowed it to send enciphered communications to terrorist cells and to track US photographic reconnaissance satellites.

Today, terrorists and drug traffickers from the jungles of Colombia to the streets of Western Europe employ advisers drawn from the intelligence services of the former Soviet Union, East Germany, and Yugoslavia and use criminals of various kinds to bribe or terrorize their opponents and protect their organizations. Accordingly, since the end of the Cold War, the targets of intelligence activity have been just as likely non-state actors as states. Operations against such organizations require smaller and more-flexible intelligence services that combine technical intelligence (that is, imagery and signals intelligence) and human intelligence; operations officers and analysts; and various military, intelligence, and security organizations.

CHAPTER THREE

NATIONAL INTELLIGENCE SYSTEMS

Nearly every country has an internal security or police force that acts as an intelligence agency on internal problems. After World War II, intelligence gathering was turned to international matters as well. During the Cold War, however, some national intelligence systems grew beyond their optimal size. Furthermore, some countries had difficulty controlling their intelligence systems. As technology enables intelligence systems to grow in power and autonomy, other bodies of government must be prepared to control them.

The intelligence systems of three countries—the United States, the Soviet Union, and the United Kingdom—have served as general models for most other intelligence organizations. The American system was adopted by many of the countries in the West. Before the collapse of communism in 1989, intelligence agencies in Eastern Europe were modeled upon those of the Soviet Union. The United Kingdom's intelligence system has served as a model for most countries with parliamentary governments.

UNITED STATES

After World War II, the United States recognized its growing need for a central organization for defense. However, there was intense debate about how much centralization was needed. The outcome was a compromise that created the CIA but allowed other departments and agencies to retain their own intelligence sections. Since then, the idea of a single intelligence system has given way to the concept of an "intelligence community." The American intelligence community includes the CIA, the Federal Bureau of Investigation (FBI), the National Security Agency (NSA), the Defense Intelligence Agency (DIA), and State Department intelligence.

The J. Edgar Hoover Building in Washington, DC, is the headquarters of the FBI.

Of these organizations, only the FBI is supposed to operate only within the United States, although it has operated abroad secretly on occasion. It deals with matters of treason, sabotage, espionage, and other threats to national internal security. It also investigates most violations of federal law, including crimes such as bank robbery, kidnapping, drug dealing, and hijacking.

An arm of the Justice Department, the FBI was founded in 1908 as the Bureau of Investigation. Its name was changed in 1935. Its present status as the most effective crime-fighting force in the world is the result mainly of the efforts of J. Edgar Hoover, who was FBI director from 1924 until his death in 1972. The Bureau is headquartered in Washington, DC, and has more than fifty field offices located in large cities throughout the United States.

The CIA was created in 1947 under the National Security Act. Since its inception, the CIA has performed three basic tasks: foreign intelligence gathering and evaluation, overseas counterintelligence operations, and secret political operations and psychological warfare in foreign countries. The CIA is headed by a director appointed by the president. It has five major divisions: the Directorate of Analysis, the Directorate of Operations, the Directorate of Science and Technology, the Directorate of Support, and the Directorate of Digital Innovation. The Directorate of Analysis is made up mostly

of research analysts who examine intelligence collected from all available open and covert sources. The Directorate of Operations is responsible for secret operations abroad. The Directorate of Science and Technology is

CIA headquarters is located in Langley, Virginia, just outside of Washington, DC.

NATIONAL SECURITY ACT

The National Security Act is a US law that reorganized the structure of the US armed forces following World War II. It was signed into law by President Harry S. Truman in July 1947. The act created the office of Secretary of Defense to oversee the country's military. It also established the National Security Council (NSC) and separate departments for each branch of the armed forces. It provided for the coordination of the military with other departments and agencies of the government concerned with national security, such as the CIA, and for presidential and congressional oversight with respect to matters of national intelligence.

The National Security Act made several organizational changes. It combined the Department of War and the Navy Department to create the Department of Defense, which also included the Departments of the Army and Air Force. The reorganization was intended to create a clear and direct line of command for all military services. The act also placed great emphasis on the coordination of national security with the intelligence community. Most notably, the legislation created the CIA and established the position of director of central intelligence, who manages the CIA and oversees the entire intelligence community. The National Security Act also established the National Security Council (NSC) to assist in the coordination of the nation's security assets.

responsible for keeping the agency aware of scientific and technological advances and for carrying out technical operations. The Directorate of Support handles the CIA's finances and personnel matters. It also contains the Office of Security, which is responsible for the security of personnel, facilities, and information as well as for uncovering spies within the CIA. The Directorate of Digital Innovation was launched in 2015 to provide CIA analysts with the latest information technology (IT) tools to aid their investigations.

Following the September 11 terrorist attacks in 2001, the United States passed the Homeland Security Act (2002). As a result, CIA analysts were integrated into the intelligence sections of the new Department of Homeland Security. The CIA and the FBI began coordinating efforts more closely. A new post, the director of national intelligence, became responsible for coordinating the various intelligence agencies and acting as the president's main adviser on intelligence.

The NSA, created in 1952, is the largest and most secret of the American intelligence organizations. Its chief function is signals intelligence—to devise and break codes and ciphers. From its headquarters near Washington, DC, the NSA conducts a variety of electronic espionage activities. Many of its activities make use of sophisticated listening devices placed on planes and ships and in ground installations overseas. The NSA's mission also includes flagging and intercepting

US director of national intelligence James R. Clapper Jr. *(center)* reviews information with US senator John McCain and US Army Lt. General Ronald L. Burgess Jr.

email, telephone, and text messages containing certain keywords. The NSA remained virtually unknown to the public until 2013, when a former computer security contractor, Edward Snowden, leaked classified information about NSA surveillance programs, drawing much attention to the organization.

The DIA, established in 1961 by the Department of Defense, performs for military intelligence much the same work that the CIA does for the executive branch of the government. In addition to the DIA, each branch of the armed services has its own intelligence units.

Astride the whole intelligence apparatus in the United States sits the National Security Council (NSC). Created by the National Security Act, it is not itself an investigative agency. It functions, rather, as part of the Executive Office of the President to sift through and integrate policies on domestic, foreign, and military matters with regard to national security. Its members are the president, vice president, secretary of state, secretary of defense, and a specially appointed national security adviser.

RUSSIA AND THE SOVIET UNION

In the Soviet Union, the Committee for State Security, or KGB (Komitet Gosudarstvennoy Bezopasnosti), combined the functions of foreign intelligence, counterintelligence, and domestic security. The KGB was established in 1954, but it had its origins in the Cheka, a secret police organization founded in 1917. It was successively called the OGPU (Unified State Political Administration), the NKVD (People's Commissariat for Internal Affairs), and the MGB (Ministry of State Security). Cheka and its successors were set up to combat counterrevolution and sabotage and to ferret out dissent and political unrest. With the onset of the Cold War, the scope of the KGB was broadened to include intelligence gathering and covert activities around the world.

Photographed in the early 1960s, KGB headquarters (commonly called the Lubyanka) was located in the heart of Moscow. Today, the building is the headquarters of Russia's Federal Security Service.

Less well known, but larger and better funded, was the Soviet military intelligence organization, GRU (Central Intelligence Office). Its main efforts were directed to stealing industrial, technological, and scientific secrets from other countries. The GRU also operated an elite corps of troops trained to fight sabotage and terrorism.

After the dissolution of the Soviet Union in 1991, the KGB was dissolved. Nevertheless, Russia's intelligence and counterintelligence services remain substantial. Especially notable is the Federal Security Service (FSB), which is responsible for internal security and counter-intelligence. Since the end of the Cold War, Russian intelligence services have continued to recruit and place spies in the CIA and the FBI. Nevertheless, Russian intelligence in general suffers from organizational issues, including the problem that the information it produces is not always properly analyzed or acted upon.

UNITED KINGDOM

British intelligence was organized along modern lines as early as the reign of Queen Elizabeth I. Compared to the intelligence agencies of the United States and the former Soviet Union, those of the United Kingdom have kept a higher degree of secrecy concerning their oper-ations. The two main British agencies are the Secret Intelligence Service (SIS), often called MI6, and the British Security Service (BSS), called MI5. The labels come from the fact that the Secret Intelligence Service was once "section six" of military intelligence and the Security Service "section five." The British services are

MI6 headquarters overlooks the Thames River in London, England.

much smaller than those of either the United States or Russia.

MI6 is a civilian organization that operates in much the same way as the American CIA. It is charged with

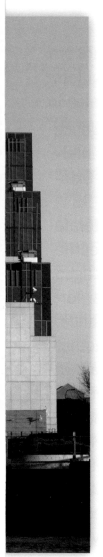

gathering information overseas and with other strategic intelligence ranging from foreign espionage to secretive political intervention abroad. Its director, who is commonly referred to as "C," is an almost anonymous figure. A high wall of secrecy likewise surrounds the rest of the organization; indeed, the British government barely acknowledges its existence.

MI5 is comparable to the American FBI, but it differs from the FBI in that it does counterintelligence work in other countries. MI5's primary responsibility is to protect British secrets at home from foreign spies and to prevent domestic sabotage, subversion, and the theft of state secrets. The service is headed by a director general, who reports to the prime minister. The director general's traditional code name is "K."

Great Britain also has a military intelligence agency called Defense Intelligence. Similar in function to the American DIA, it coordinates the information-gathering work of the armed service branches. Electronic surveillance is carried out by the Government Communications Headquarters (GCHQ). The work of all the British intelligence agencies is coordinated by the Joint Intelligence Committee, which is part of the Cabinet Office.

Yuval Diskin, director of the Israeli intelligence service Shin Bet from 2005 to 2011, addresses the Foreign Affairs and Defense Committee of the Israeli Knesset (Parliament) on January 3, 2006.

as Mossad, carries out foreign espionage and covert political and paramilitary operations, including the assassination of Palestinian terrorists and other figures. Its head reports directly to the prime minister.

Shin Bet, which takes its name from the Hebrew initials for General Security Services, conducts internal counterintelligence. Its focus is potential sabotage, terrorist activities, and security matters of a strongly political nature. In the 1980s and 1990s, Shin Bet's reputation was affected by a series of scandals, including its use of torture against Palestinian detainees and its role in the assassinations of alleged Palestinian militants.

A third major Israeli intelligence organization is Military Intelligence, commonly called Aman. Some observers view it as a rival to Mossad, and conflicts between the two agencies have been reported. Its chief is the military intelligence adviser to the minister of defense.

GERMANY

Following the division of Germany after World War II, West Germany created a loosely organized intelligence community overseen by a parliamentary committee. The Federal Intelligence Service (Bundesnachrichtendienst, or BND) is responsible primarily for foreign intelligence. Its staff was cut down greatly after West and East Germany reunified. The Federal Office for the Protection of the Constitution (Bundesamt für Verfassungsshutz, or BfV) is charged with protecting the internal security of the country. Additionally, each German state performs similar counterintelligence operations through a separate State Office for the Protection of the Constitution (Landesbehörden für Verfassungsschutz, or LfV). During the Cold War, West German intelligence was plagued with scandals, often involving the defection of senior officers to East Germany and the Soviet Union.

During the 1990s the German intelligence services were widely criticized for their failure to infiltrate militant Islamic groups.

East Germany's Ministry of State Security (Ministerium für Staatssicherheit, or MfS) was one of the largest intelligence and security services in the world. Known as the Stasi by East Germans, it used some 90,000 regular employees—and nearly double that number of informers—to watch the country's 17 million people. Stasi foreign intelligence successfully penetrated the West German armed forces, intelligence services, and political parties. All observers agree that the East Germans won the intelligence Cold War in Germany.

Since the reunification of Germany in 1990, the German intelligence and security services have embraced the principles of democratic West Germany and have been reduced in size.

OTHER NOTABLE INTELLIGENCE SYSTEMS

While the aforementioned countries have boasted the largest and best-organized international intelligence operations, many other countries' intelligence services have served influential roles in domestic and regional politics. For instance, the Cuban Ministry of the Interior (MININT) has lent substantial support to liberation movements throughout Latin America and Africa and maintains an intelligence network within Cuban communities in the United States. Colombia's counterintelligence and security services are notable for their role in the country's decades-long war against Marxist guerrilla groups and drug traffickers.

In the Middle East, Iraq under Saddam Hussein maintained extensive intelligence operations to protect

Some intelligence organizations, such as Iran's Revolutionary Guards, play a role in running a country's affairs and enforcing government policy.

the regime from internal and foreign enemies and to collect information on the construction of weapons of mass destruction. Iran's Revolutionary Guards, or Pasdaran, has been influential in running the country's affairs and enforcing the government's Islamic code of morality in addition to gathering intelligence and conducting secret operations. The intelligence operations of Pakistan's Inter-Service Intelligence (ISI) have included the funding and training of Afghan fighters during Afghanistan's guerrilla war against the Soviet Union in the 1980s and the arming and training of the Taliban movement before the September 11 terrorist attacks against the United States. India's intelligence community—which, unlike many, is accountable to the civilian government—carries out operations in the Indian subcontinent, including in Bangladesh, Sri Lanka, and Pakistan.

Perhaps the clearest remnant of Cold War–era intelligence practices persists on the Korean peninsula. South Korea's intelligence community, which was established in the 1960s with US guidance, was once deeply involved in domestic politics and human rights abuses, especially in the 1980s. In the 1990s, the country's main intelligence agency, now known as the National Intelligence Service (NIS), was reformed. The NIS and the Defense Security Command are responsible for the collection of national security intelligence, particularly with regard to the threat from North Korea. Far less is known about North Korea's intelligence community. Operations are apparently controlled by the Cabinet General Intelligence Bureau, a component of the Central Committee of the ruling Korean Workers' (Communist) Party. A semisecret organization known as the General Association of Korean Residents in Japan (Chosen Soren) collects information, funds, and technology from citizens living abroad. North Korea also has a large military intelligence system. During the Cold War, the country undertook violent covert action, including the assassination of South Korean officials and the

The Chosen Soren, based in Tokyo, is the association of Koreans living in Japan. The organization's intelligence work has been pivotal in helping North Korea to acquire advanced technology.

sabotage of a South Korean airliner. Since the 1990s, North Korea has made efforts to land agents in South Korea from fishing trawlers and submarines and through tunnels bored under the countries' shared border.

South Africa has the most extensive and effective intelligence community of all African countries. During the apartheid era, its military intelligence supported and trained guerrilla movements in Angola, Zimbabwe, and Mozambique. Its domestic efforts placed agents in black communities, arrested dissidents, and assassinated real and suspected enemies of the government. After the end of apartheid in 1994, the South African intelligence system was greatly reformed. Nonetheless, it is still the only service in Africa capable of conducting widespread operations outside the region.

CHAPTER FOUR

MILITARY INTELLIGENCE

Military intelligence is as old as warfare itself. Since ancient times, intelligence has served a valuable role in the planning and execution of military operations. Today, countries have the ability to gather and produce intelligence more rapidly and more accurately than ever before. Satellites, ultramodern aircraft, electronic systems, human sources, cameras, imaging and electronic devices, and a host of other systems permit the amassing of information on a scale that was unheard of in the past.

LEVELS OF MILITARY INTELLIGENCE

Military operations rely on both strategic and tactical intelligence. Strategic intelligence is used to formulate policy and military plans at the international and national policy levels. Tactical intelligence responds to the needs of military field commanders so they can plan for and, if necessary, conduct combat operations.

Whether tactical or strategic, military intelligence attempts to respond to or satisfy the needs of the operational leader, the person who has to act or react to a given set of circumstances. The process begins when the commander determines what information is needed to act responsibly. Several terms are used when discussing

US officers study cartographic intelligence prior to a military operation outside Baghdad, Iraq, on July 5, 2007.

these requirements. On the national level they are usually called the essential elements of information and are defined as those items of intelligence information about a foreign power, armed force, target, or physical environment that are absolutely vital for timely and accurate decision making. On the tactical level, intelligence needs are defined in a similar manner; often called information requirements, they are those items of information concerning the enemy and his environment that must be collected and processed in order to meet the intelligence needs of the military commander.

SOURCES OF MILITARY INTELLIGENCE

It is critical for the intelligence analyst to know the source of information. Depending on the nature of a problem, certain sources are of great value and are therefore considered of high quality, while other sources, although contributing to the production of intelligence, are supportive rather than critical in nature.

ACOUSTICS

This is information derived from analyzing acoustic waves that are radiated either intentionally or unintentionally. In naval intelligence, underwater acoustic waves from surface ships and submarines are detected by sonar arrays. These sensors are extremely accurate and are a major source of information on submarines in the world's oceans.

IMAGERY

This is information gleaned from analyzing all types of imagery, including photography as well as infrared and ultraviolet imagery. The examination of imagery, called imagery interpretation, is the process of locating, recognizing, identifying, and describing objects, activities, and terrain that appear on imagery.

Imagery collected by satellites and high-altitude aircraft is one of the most important sources of intelligence. It not only provides information for a huge number of intelligence categories (such as order of battle, military operations, scientific and technical developments, and economics), but it is indispensable for successfully monitoring compliance with arms-limitation treaties. The Intermediate Nuclear Forces Treaty of 1987 allowed the United States to periodically request that the Soviet Union open certain intercontinental ballistic missile sites so that US satellites (referred to as "national technical means") could verify that the sites did not house intermediate-range missiles banned by the treaty.

Tactical infrared imaging devices can often identify camouflaged tanks and armor because the materials used to cover them—trees, branches, and leaves—

The Northrop Grumman RQ-4 Global Hawk is an unmanned aircraft used by the US Air Force to relay intelligence, surveillance, and reconnaissance data to fighting units on the ground.

often register different infrared signatures than does the surrounding foliage. Infrared satellites can register heat through clouds, producing imagery on enemy forces, equipment, and movements.

SIGNALS

Gained from intercepting, processing, and analyzing foreign electrical communications and other signals, signals intelligence (often called SIGINT) comprises three elements: communications, electronics, and telemetry.

Communications intelligence is gleaned from foreign communications that are intercepted by someone other than the intended recipients. Such intelligence can be of the greatest value to a nation's fighting forces because it allows them to be privy to the strategies, weaknesses, and attitudes of the enemy. For example, before and during World War II, the US Navy's breaking of the Japanese PURPLE code allowed the United States to know of Japanese moves in advance. It even provided warning of the attack on Pearl Harbor, although this intelligence was not sent to Hawaii quickly enough to prevent the debacle.

Electronics intelligence (also called ELINT) is technical and intelligence information obtained from foreign electromagnetic emissions that are not radiated by communications equipment or by nuclear detonations and radioactive sources. By analyzing the electronic emissions from a given weapon or electronic system, an intelligence analyst can very often determine the purpose of the device.

Telemetry intelligence is technical information that is derived from intercepting, processing, and analyzing foreign telemetry data. For example, by intercepting the telemetry signals emitted during foreign ballistic missile tests, an intelligence agency can calculate the range, accuracy, and number of warheads of the weapon.

RADIATION

This source of intelligence does not include energy emanating from nuclear detonations or radioactive sources. Rather, it concerns unintentional emissions of energy from electronic systems (while ELINT is based on intentional radiations from the same systems). Inadequate shielding of electronic systems, or the following of incorrect procedures, may result in inadvertent energy emissions, which, when analyzed, may reveal a great deal about a system's purpose or capabilities.

FOREIGN MATÉRIEL

In 1976, a Soviet air force lieutenant, wishing to defect to the West, flew a MiG-25 Foxbat to Japan, where Japanese and US technicians pored over every detail of the supersonic fighter before reassembling it and handing it back to its owners. Such analysis of a foreign weapon system can prove invaluable in producing systems to defeat it, and intelligence derived from any foreign matériel is of great value in assessing enemy capabilities.

HUMAN AGENTS

Often called HUMINT, human intelligence is provided by people rather than by technical means and is very often provided by spies and covert agents. Spies are often a prime source of information about a nation's political leaders, strategies, and political decisions. The Soviet colonel Oleg Penkovsky, for example, was a very important source for British and US intelligence until he was arrested and executed in 1963. The political, scientific, and technical information he provided included data on the capabilities of Soviet intermediate-range missiles during the Cuban missile crisis. Similarly, the Philby–Burgess–Maclean spy ring, which penetrated the highest circles of Britain's MI6 intelligence agency, provided the Soviets with a tremendous amount of

In 1953, Julius and Ethel Rosenberg became the first US civilians to be put to death for espionage. They were convicted of providing information about nuclear weapons to the Soviet Union.

WHISTLE-BLOWERS IN THE MILITARY

Analysts working in military intelligence often have access to classified information, and at times intelligence officers have chosen to expose military secrets. "Whistle-blowing" is the term used to characterize the activities of individuals who, without authorization, reveal private or classified information about military operations, usually related to wrongdoing or misconduct. Whistle-blowers generally state that such actions are motivated by a commitment to the public interest.

One notable whistle-blower was Daniel Ellsberg, an American military analyst who, in 1971, leaked portions of a classified 7,000-page report that detailed the history of US intervention in Indochina from World War II until 1968. Dubbed the Pentagon Papers, the document appeared to undercut the publicly stated justification of the Vietnam War. Ellsberg was charged under the Espionage Act, and the charges he faced could have resulted in up to 115 years in prison. His trial, which began in January 1973, lasted four months and ended with the dismissal of all charges after evidence of governmental misconduct came to light.

Also noteworthy is Chelsea Manning, a US Army intelligence analyst who in 2009–2010 provided the website WikiLeaks with hundreds of thousands of classified documents in what was believed to be the largest unauthorized release of state secrets in US history. In May 2010, Manning was arrested. She ultimately was charged with more than two dozen offenses, including the capital offense of aiding the enemy. In July 2013, Manning was found not guilty of aiding the enemy but was convicted of numerous other counts, including espionage and theft. The following month Manning was sentenced to thirty-five years in prison.

information on British and Allied military and counterintelligence operations during and after World War II. In the United States, the Walker family sold the Soviet Union classified reports on the tracking of Soviet submarines and surface ships. Operating from 1968 until it was broken up in 1985, this spy ring did irreparable damage to the submarine warfare capabilities of the US Navy.

TYPES OF MILITARY INTELLIGENCE

In most situations, intelligence production involves the assessment of conflicting pieces of incomplete information, the attempt to determine the correct items, and then the processing and assembly of these accurate items into a complete, understandable document that responds to the needs of the operational leader. More often than not the resulting product, which is usually called an intelligence appraisal or intelligence assessment, contains some incorrect information.

In order to structure this production, analysts divide intelligence into types. While all types of intelligence are valuable, in any given situation some may be of greater worth than others, may be more accurate, and may provide a more complete view of the situation. By dividing intelligence into types, analysts and commanders arrive at a better understanding of the value and accuracy of a given piece of information.

ARMED FORCES

Information on a potential enemy's armed forces—that is, personnel, training, equipment, bases, capabilities, manpower levels, disposition, readiness, and other factors pertaining to strength and effectiveness—is crucial for a nation that is about to enter combat. If the weaknesses can be exploited, then the conflict may be won more quickly and with fewer casualties. Toward the end of World War II, owing to incomplete intelligence, it was predicted that Japan would fight resolutely against a US invasion and that the United States might suffer up to one million casualties. This was a major factor in the decision to drop atomic bombs on Hiroshima and Nagasaki. In reality, though, Japanese resolve was grossly overestimated, and Japan could probably have been conquered with far fewer Allied casualties.

BIOGRAPHICAL

This is information collected on the views, traits, habits, skills, importance, relationships, health, and professional history of the leaders and important individuals of a nation. Biographical intelligence is important to those who must decide whether to support a foreign leader. For example, when Fidel Castro first came to power in Cuba in 1959, he claimed to be a nationalist and was even allowed to conduct a speaking tour in the United States. Subsequently, however, Castro revealed that he was a communist who intended to transform Cuba into a Soviet-style state. More accurate intelligence on Castro might have revealed his intentions more promptly, and US foreign policy could have been revised accordingly.

In clandestine operations, one of the most difficult problems is assessing the validity of an individual who volunteers his services to an intelligence organization. Very often, information on the family life, education, travels, and professional and political affiliations of such a person provides great insight into motivation and can help in verifying authenticity.

CARTOGRAPHIC

Derived from maps and charts, cartographic intelligence is crucial for all military operations. During the

Falkland Islands War of 1982, for example, British forces depended heavily on cartography. They also interviewed schoolteachers and scientists who had recently left the islands so that they had the most accurate information possible on road conditions, towns, and facilities. This prepared invading troops to meet the obstacles caused by rough terrain and poor roads, and as a result the invasion went remarkably well.

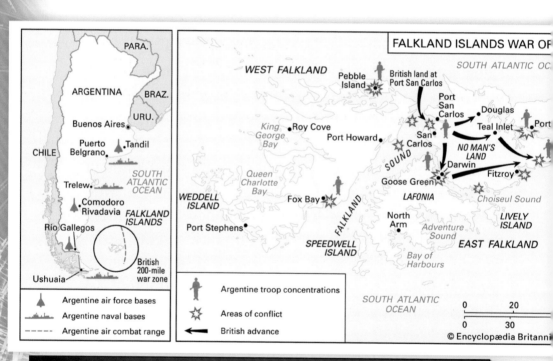

Cartographic intelligence proved vital to British success in the Falkland Islands War of 1982. With knowledge of the islands' physical features and roads, British forces successfully invaded and defeated Argentine troops.

ECONOMIC

This is information concerning the production, distribution, and consumption of goods and services, as well as labor, finance, taxation, and other aspects of a nation's economy or of the international economic system. Economic intelligence allows a nation to estimate the magnitude of possible military threats and is also valuable in estimating the intentions of a potential enemy. In wartime, economic intelligence is a prime indicator of an enemy's ability to sustain a war. This is particularly important when analyzing small nations, such as Israel, where a conflict requires total mobilization and cannot be sustained for long without creating severe economic problems.

ENERGY

Energy intelligence specifically addresses the location and size of foreign energy resources; how these resources are used and allocated; foreign governments' energy policies, plans, and programs; new or improved foreign energy technologies; and the economic and security aspects of foreign energy supply, demand, production, distribution, and use.

Energy requirements can be an important factor in military planning. For example, as German forces were advancing on Moscow during World War II,

Hitler, on being informed that the German military was short of fuel, sent several of the advancing units southward to capture the oil complexes at Baku on the Caspian Sea. This move so depleted the forces advancing on Moscow that they failed to capture the city, dealing the German war effort a fatal setback. Later, on the Western Front, advancing Allied forces were so short of fuel that US general George Patton's 3rd Army was forced to stop and await replenishment. This allowed the retreating Germans to dig in and prolong the war.

COUNTERINTELLIGENCE

Counterintelligence is intended to detect, counteract, and prevent espionage and other clandestine intelligence activities, sabotage, terrorist attacks, or assassinations conducted on behalf of foreign powers, organizations, or persons. It is especially vital that nations identify the capabilities and intentions of international terrorist organizations so that their operations can be thwarted. In the event that a terrorist attack is successful, identifying the culprit allows for reprisals, which are crucial to combating terrorism.

In December 1988, an American commercial aircraft was destroyed over Scotland, and neither the
United States nor Great Britain initially could identify the terrorist organization involved. As a result,
the act was successful from the perspective of the

Because of the complexity of the investigation, neither US nor British counterintelligence could initially identify the terrorists responsible for the bombing of Pan Am Flight 103 over Lockerbie, Scotland, in 1988. A Libyan intelligence agent was eventually convicted of the bombing in 2001.

terrorists, who had injured their enemy without suffering retaliation.

GEOGRAPHIC

Gained from studying natural characteristics including terrain, climate, natural resources, transportation, boundaries, and population distribution, military geographic intelligence involves evaluating all such factors that in any way influence military operations.

Geographic intelligence was crucial to the success of Israel's rescue mission at the Entebbe airport in Uganda in 1976. Because they had reliable information on the exact location of the buildings at the airport, of the roads leading to Entebbe, and of military bases in the region, Israeli soldiers were able to land in three transport planes, kill many of the terrorists holding Israeli hostages, and depart with most of the hostages before the Ugandan military could react. A significant factor in the disastrous US attempt to rescue its hostages in Iran in 1980 was a failure to anticipate and prepare for seasonal sandstorms, which disabled several helicopters and forced the rescuers to abort their mission.

MEDICAL

This is intelligence gained from studying every aspect of foreign natural and man-made environments that could affect the health of military forces. This information can be used not only to predict the medical weaknesses of an enemy but also to provide one's own forces with adequate medical protection. For example, in the Spanish-American War of 1898, the majority of US casualties in the Caribbean resulted from disease rather than combat, because US forces were not prepared to deal with the environment of that region.

SOCIOLOGICAL

Information on a nation's social stratification, value systems, beliefs, and other social characteristics are of crucial value in assessing nations where national, racial, or social factions can have a great impact on a nation's military capability.

A lack of good sociological intelligence was a major cause of US blunders in dealing with revolutionary Iran. When Mohammad Reza Shah Pahlavi was overthrown in 1979, the United States had only the most superficial understanding of Islam and Iranian society, and the situation improved only slightly in subsequent years. As a result, the United States often remained ignorant about Iranian officials, calling them "radical" or "moderate" even when such terms did more to cloud a situation than to make it clear.

Better sociological intelligence could have eased tensions between the United States and post-revolution Iran. Shown here, American hostages are taken at the US Embassy in Tehran during the Iran hostage crisis (1979–1981).

TRANSPORTATION AND TELECOMMUNICATION

This type of intelligence can be crucial to correctly assessing a nation's ability to wage war, as it concerns a nation's

highways, railroads, inland water-ways, and civil airways as well as its information systems and broadcast capabilities. When China sent troops across the border into Vietnam in 1979, many observers assumed that China would win the conflict. This estimate was based on the huge size of the Chinese army and on its excellent performance against United Nations forces in the Korean War. After China failed to score a decisive victory, the same commentators examined China's transportation and telecommunication networks and found that, while they were very highly developed in the Northeast, they were quite primitive in the South. It was concluded that the advanced northeastern systems and the primitive southern systems were prime factors in China's success in Korea and in its lackluster performance in Vietnam.

Perhaps the earliest codification of intelligence doctrine can be found in *The Art of War*, a fifth-century BCE military treatise by the Chinese strategist Sunzi. Sunzi stressed the importance of establishing a robust intelligence operation, going so far as to identify the types of agents that should be recruited. This advice was centuries ahead of its time, and Western leaders would not be in a position to pursue such ends until the rise of the modern nation-state. Queen Elizabeth I's spymaster, Sir Francis Walsingham, would craft one of the earliest intelligence operations in Europe, and his expert use of counterintelligence frustrated England's enemies at every turn.

Many of the strategies employed by Sunzi and Walsingham remain standard operating procedure. Operation Mincemeat, an elaborate British World War II operation that deceived Nazi commanders into believing that an Allied attack was to be launched on Greece instead of Sicily, was in many ways similar to a disinformation campaign waged by Walsingham in advance of Sir Francis Drake's surprise raid on Cádiz, Spain, in April 1587. In both cases, spies preyed upon the greed or gullibility of unknowing accomplices to lend credibility to their false narratives. Despite the increasing role of computers in data harvesting and analysis, such human weaknesses—and the ability to identify and capitalize on them—will ensure that classic spy craft remains a crucial element in the intelligence game for years to come.

TIMELINE

5TH CENTURY BCE The Chinese military strategist Sunzi composes the war and military treatise *Bingfa* (*The Art of War*).

16TH CENTURY CE England, France, and other European countries begin developing extensive intelligence systems.

1866 Under Wilhelm Stieber, the Foreign Office Political Field Police, the first large-scale espionage organization, is formed in Prussia.

1914 World War I begins, largely as a result of intelligence failures during the buildup to the war.

1917 British intelligence deciphers the "Zimmermann Note," leading the United States to enter World War I.

1917 The Bolshevik intelligence organization Cheka is established.

1920s European nations (especially Italy, Germany, and the Soviet Union) begin greatly expanding their international intelligence operations.

1942 The United States creates the Office of Strategic Services (OSS).

1945 The Cold War, during which intelligence would become one of the world's largest industries, begins.

1947 The United States passes the National Security Act, which establishes the National Security

Council (NSC) and the Central Intelligence Agency (CIA).

1954 The Soviet Union establishes the KGB.

1971 American military analyst Daniel Ellsberg leaks the Pentagon Papers, undermining public support for US involvement in Vietnam.

1989 The Cold War ends, and many intelligence organizations reform or shift focus to non-state actors.

1994 CIA official Aldrich Ames is convicted of having sold American intelligence information to the Soviet Union and Russia.

1996 Harold J. Nicholson of the CIA is arrested for spying for Russia.

2001 The September 11 terrorist attacks against the United States make counterterrorism a top priority of intelligence operations.

2002 The United States passes the Homeland Security Act, which creates the Department of Homeland Security.

2010 WikiLeaks publishes military documents obtained from US intelligence analyst Chelsea Manning, the largest unauthorized release of state secrets in US history.

GLOSSARY

AGENT A person who tries to get secret information about another country, government, etc.

APARTHEID South Africa's policy of racial segregation and discrimination against the country's nonwhite majority for most of the second half of the twentieth century.

ATTACHÉ A person who works at an embassy as an expert on a particular subject.

AUTONOMY The state of being self-governing.

BUREAUCRACY A body of nonelective government officials.

CIPHER A method of transforming a text in order to conceal its meaning.

CLANDESTINE Marked by, held in, or conducted with secrecy.

COLD WAR The ideological conflict between the United States and the Soviet Union and their respective allies following World War II.

COUNTERINTELLIGENCE Organized activity of an intelligence service designed to block an enemy's sources of information, to deceive the enemy, to prevent sabotage, and to gather political and military information.

COUP A sudden attempt by a small group of people to take over a government usually through violence; also called coup d'état.

COVERT Made, shown, or done in a way that is not easily seen or noticed; secret or hidden.

DIRECTORATE An executive staff (as of a department).

ENCIPHER To convert (a message) into cipher.

ESPIONAGE The practice of spying or using spies to obtain information about the plans and activities especially of a foreign government or a competing company.

EXPENDABLE More easily or economically replaced than rescued, salvaged, or protected.

MATÉRIEL Military equipment and supplies.

NATIONALISM Loyalty and devotion to a nation, especially as expressed in the glorifying of one nation above all others.

OBSOLETE No longer in use or no longer useful.

PARLIAMENTARY GOVERNMENT A system of government having the real executive power vested in a cabinet composed of members of the legislature who are individually and collectively responsible to the legislature.

RECONNAISSANCE Military activity in which soldiers, airplanes, etc., are sent to find out information about an enemy.

STRATEGIC Of or relating to a general plan that is

created to achieve a goal in war, politics, etc., usually over a long period of time.

SURVEILLANCE The act of carefully watching someone or something, especially in order to prevent or detect a crime.

TACTICAL Of, relating to, or used for a specific plan that is created to achieve a particular goal in war, politics, etc.

FOR MORE INFORMATION

Canadian Security Intelligence Service (CSIS)
PO Box 9732 Station T
Ottawa, ON K1G 4G4
Canada
(613) 993-9620
Website: https://www.csis-scrs.gc.ca/index-en.php
    The CSIS is Canada's intelligence service dedi-
    cated to counterterrorism and law enforcement.
    Its artifact collection—which contains surveillance
    and tradecraft artifacts from the Cold War era—
    can be explored online.

CIA Museum
Central Intelligence Agency
Office of Public Affairs
Washington, DC 20505
(703) 482-0623
Website: https://www.cia.gov/about-cia/cia-museum/
    experience-the-collection
    The CIA Museum hosts artifacts—including cloth-
    ing, equipment, and weapons—formerly used by
    the CIA, its predecessor the OSS, and foreign intel-
    ligence agencies. Though the museum is not open
    to the public, its collection is accessible online.

The Cold War Museum
PO Box 861526
7142 Lineweaver Road

Vint Hill, VA 20187

(540) 341-2008

Website: http://www.coldwar.org

The Cold War Museum is a nonprofit organization dedicated to documenting and preserving the history of the Cold War. Its website includes numerous online exhibits and a timeline of the Cold War.

Electronic Frontier Foundation (EFF)

815 Eddy Street

San Francisco, CA 94109

(415) 436-9333

Website: https://www.eff.org

The EFF is a nonprofit organization dedicated to protecting internet privacy and promoting security online. It advocates against digital surveillance programs such as those of the National Security Agency and shines a spotlight on legal challenges to such efforts.

International Spy Museum

800 F Street NW

Washington, DC 20004

(202) 393-7798

Website: http://www.spymuseum.org

Opened in 2002, the International Spy Museum is the only public museum in the United States dedicated wholly to espionage. It boasts an impressive

collection of international spy artifacts and walks
visitors through the history of intelligence and
surveillance.

National Cryptologic Museum
8290 Colony Seven Road
Annapolis Junction, MD 20701
(301) 688-5849
Website: https://www.nsa.gov/about/cryptologic
_heritage/museum
Located at the National Security Agency's headquarters, the National Cryptologic Museum hosts
thousands of artifacts related to the history and
craft of cryptology. Its extensive library further pro-
motes interest and research in cryptologic history.

WEBSITES

Because of the changing nature of internet links,
Rosen Publishing has developed an online list of
websites related to the subject of this book. This
site is updated regularly. Please use this link to
access the list:

http://www.rosenlinks.com/BLAW/spy

FOR FURTHER READING

Allen, Thomas B., and Roger MacBride Allen. *Mr. Lincoln's High-Tech War: How the North Used the Telegraph, Railroads, Surveillance Balloons, Ironclads, High-Powered Weapons, and More to Win the Civil War.* Washington, DC: National Geographic, 2009.

Collard, Sneed B. *The CIA and FBI: Top Secret.* Vero Beach, FL: Rourke Educational Media, 2014.

Curley, Robert, ed. *Cryptography: Cracking Codes.* New York, NY: Britannica Educational Publishing, 2014.

Curley, Robert, ed. *Spy Agencies, Intelligence Operations, and the People Behind Them.* New York, NY: Britannica Educational Publishing, 2014.

Doak, Robin S. *National Intelligence* (Cornerstones of Freedom). New York, NY: Children's Press, 2013.

Goodman, Michael E. *The KGB and Other Russian Spies.* Mankato, MN: Creative Education, 2012.

Harmon, Daniel E. *Special Ops: Military Intelligence.* New York, NY: Rosen Publishing, 2015.

McCollum, Sean. *The CIA: The Missions.* North Mankato, MN: Capstone Press, 2013.

Senker, Cath. *Privacy and Surveillance.* New York, NY: Rosen Central, 2012.

Streissguth, Thomas. *The Security Agencies of the United States: How the CIA, FBI, NSA and Homeland Security Keep Us Safe.* Berkeley Heights, NJ: Enslow Publishers, 2013.

Thompson, Tamara. *Domestic Surveillance.* Farmington Hills, MI: Greenhaven Press, 2015.

Woog, Adam. *Careers in the FBI.* New York, NY: Cavendish Square Publishing, 2014.

INDEX